Driving Late to the Party
The Kansas Poems

Jeff Worley

Driving Late to the Party
The Kansas Poems

Jeff Worley

WOODLEY PRESS

Editor: Israel Wasserstein
Copyright ©2012 Jeff Worley
Back cover photo by Frank Stephenson
Printed by Lightning Source
Cover and book design by Leah Sewell
          lsewell.tumblr.com/

Woodley Press
Department of English
Washburn University
Topeka, KS 66621
http://www.washburn.edu/reference/woodley-press/

ISBN: 978-0-9854586-76-9

ACKNOWLEDGMENTS

Some of these poems were published in two books from Mid-List Press: *The Only Time There Is* and *Happy Hour at the Two Keys Tavern*. I'd also like to thank the editors of the following magazines and journals, in which these poems, sometimes in different versions, first appeared:

Atlanta Review: "Burnout," "On My 13th Birthday . . ."
Black Warrior Review: "Sin," "Skunk"
College English: "After the Move Back to Wichita"
Connecticut Review: "Mr. Peanut"
Florida Review: "Seminal Statement"
Green Mountains Review: "Cheryl Leigh, I Think Her Name Was," "Europe on $5 a Day"
Images: "Driving Late to the Party"
Kansas Quarterly. "Loaded"
The Literary Review: "So You Want to Be a Teaching Assistant in English"
Mikrokosmos: "When I Heard the News"
The Minnesota Review: "Starting Point"
The Missouri Review: "Joy"
New Letters: "Embracing the Literal"
Northeast: "During a Zen Reading My Libido Acts Up Again"
Poet & Critic: "Legacy"
Poetry East: "Fishing Lesson from My Father"
Poetry Northwest: "December 24, 1959," "Soft Landings"
Rattle: "How to Become a Professional Folk Singer"
River Styx: "Letter I Never Sent My Father," "Last at Bat, Texas League Playoffs, 1961"
The Southern Review: "Boeing Print Shop," "Sleeping with Two Women"
Tampa Review: "Out with the Boys, 1969," "My Senior Yearbook Photo"
Witness: "First Job, Griff's Burger Bar," "Here Is My Father"
Zone 3: "For Miles Abrams, Appearing Tonight in Kansas City"

An earlier version of "My Mother's 85th Birthday," titled "Spoons," appeared in *The Beloit Poetry Journal*.

"So You Want to Be a Teaching Assistant in English" was reprinted in *Mikrokosmos* and also appeared on the Web site Verse Daily (www.versedaily.org).

"Fishing Lesson from My Father" also appeared in *Atlanta Review*.

"After the Move Back to Wichita" was reprinted in the anthology *Motif: All the Livelong Day*.

 CONTENTS

I.

II.

III.

for Gaylord Lynn Dold,
simpatico companion
on the long ride

 I.

SEMINAL STATEMENT

When I lay curled inside my mother,
    like a little hieroglyph,
        I know she moved

with an obverse grace,
    feeling the first dark
        tuber growing.

When I shifted, I sent concentric
    circles to every inlet
        of her body.

I bobbed like a plump apple.
    I scissor-kicked, danced
        the intermittent boogaloo

we homunculi do when we hunger
    beyond sustenance
        for pure release

and the seductive light.
    She told me years later
        I became such a presence

she would search her face daily
    in the oval mirror
        for some sign of herself.

She assured me I did my best
    to yerk and sock
        my way out,

then twisted like a slick fish
    in the bright net of light.
        My father swears

he heard my bellowing richochet
        one floor down
                and along the corridor

as he sat sweating through *Life*,
        July 4th pinwheels
                palpably rising from the page.

Now I see him clearly:
        shirt pocket stuffed
                with fat cigars,

suddenly inexplicably terrified
        by what he'd set
                in motion.

Glancing again at his watch,
        the perfect circle
                strapped to his wrist

harnassing his blood and mine
        at the starting line.

STARTING POINT

The first memory isn't the stagger
from father to mother
like the photographs say.
I was five, in the Scotts' backyard
watching two chickens on a clothesline.
He tied their feet with wire
and stretched their necks down.
He struck twice with the cleaver
and tossed the heads into tall weeds.

This wasn't what moved me:
I was trying the center of the seesaw,
gliding on wood currents,
searching my body for balance.
My hands stretched into pockets of wind.
I rose like woodsmoke
over the speckled ground,
floated like a cloud, nearly invisible,
above the neighborhood until I heard

my father calling, my mother clanging
the cow bell for dinner. I fell
back to earth, to the red splattering
of stars under the clothesline, then pulled
myself up and began to follow
my human feet.

FISHING LESSON FROM MY FATHER, 1957

Did your parents encourage you to write poetry?
—a student's question

First, learn to love the quiet.
Cast out your line as if you
were invisible, a ghost here
in the morning mist
of the Little Arkansas River.
What you hope to catch is
there for you. And Jeff—
are you listening?—
you've got to be patient.
If you can't wait, then don't
unpack your tackle box.
Sometimes nothing happens.
But then—you may be half dozing
in a solid slant of light—
something will jerk you awake.
Feisty silver scales tossing beads
of water in every direction.
Reel it in,
hold it up to the light,
then let it go.

EMBRACING THE LITERAL

What did I know? What? Other than Whitley's knees
pinning me to the cold ground.
Every friend I had was screaming my name,
but I couldn't move. It was November.
His backyard was surrendering to the granite sky.
His fists pounded my chest. His voice
was the deep hollow sound of someone pissing
on mud: *Give, you cocksucker, give!*
I was ten, with no idea what a cocksucker
was, though I was certain I wasn't one.

As the circle tightened around us, my name ringing
in the air, I knew anything could happen—a split lip,
the bright coin of my blood staining the ground,
an eye punched purple . . . So when Whitley said
he was going to break off both of my arms
and feed them to his Doberman, I believed him.
I hadn't given a thought to hyperbole, or metaphor,
what they could contain and conceal . . .
So I flashed forward to the Armless Boy, the boy
who would learn to tie his shoes with his teeth,
who would walk the neighborhood with everyone watching,
tenderly, under their solid swags of gingerbread.

Then Whitley stood up, a workman
whose job was finished. I lay unbloodied
inside the circle of friends, an ebb tide
pulling slowly away. Whitley strode toward
his back door, knuckles receding in the dusk.
I was OK, my knees buckling slightly
when I stood, Whitley's Doberman
happily snoring at the end of its chain . . .

But since I'd been so eager to embrace the literal,
to give away my arms, they seemed superfluous
now. My fingers wriggled like alien creatures,
and dust began to settle on the ragged stumps of my shoulders.

DECEMBER 24, 1959

My mother shook the egg of snow
and handed it to my father,
sitting crosslegged near
the Colorado pine.
He looked at the flurry she'd made
and tossed it high, Bing Crosby
spinning us through another Christmas.
Bob! she cried, because the egg
was glass, was precious
because her mother had sent it
Special Delivery. It rose
toward the unpainted beams
of our new family room.
I quit rattling and shaking
my presents, suddenly stopped
imagining everything
I'd ever wanted
under the Daisy and Pluto paper.

And as the glass paperweight rose,
each colliding grain of fake snow
seemed to want to keep rising
through the ceiling,
into the deep Wichita sky
and on out of the world, the world
that held it and us in its close
bright wrapping. Then the snow,
the tiny plastic steeples,
the vertiginous people walking
in their one spot forever,
and the tiny eternally mute
barking dog fell into the palm
of my father's other hand,
like a clock shook loose
from the future. The snow ticking
predictably down.

SIN

When the Jehovahs bring
their long shadows up the walk,
it's Sunday. The agnostic
inside me revs up the Lawn Boy,
looks down at the next stripe
of grass. *Hell is raging below you,*
they would tell me if I'd let them.
    Half an hour ago
my neighbor Terry's Lawn Boy
sucked hell right out of the ground.
A welter of yellow jackets rode
the whirlwind up and planted
tiny electric flags in his face
and neck. I've never seen him so
happy—just now whistling
what sounds like "Amazing Grace"
and pouring unleaded into that humming
hole; one blue *whoosh* and it's over.
    Once at the Fourth of July picnic,
my 12th birthday, crazy cousin Karen
caught a bee and put it in her mouth.
Her cheeks buzzed. She swallowed.
I lay with my ear to her bare stomach
and swore I could hear the mad buzzing.
Of course my mother found us
in that position and asked what
on earth I thought I was doing.
How could I tell her the truth? So
my father walked me into the dark
woods. He told me about hell and sin
and urges I should never give in to.
Pleasures, it suddenly occurred to me
(thinking of skin so buzzingly alive),
that would surely be heaven,
right here on earth.

FOR MILES ABRAMS, APPEARING
TONIGHT IN KANSAS CITY

Every night, Miles, your house
was lit up like a riverboat.
Swing jazz trumpeted through

the windows, the fat delicious
notes floating into the warm air.
Every boy in 6th grade knew about her,

your exhibitionist mother,
Exhibit A for all of us dying
to see a woman's body, naked

and parting the air in front of us.
So there we were, half a dozen tremulous
12-year-olds crouched like Troglodytes

beneath the livingroom window,
waiting for Jeff Parker to show up
with the step ladder. For you,

your father on duty in Darmstadt,
she was the dancing dervish,
local impropriety, the hot, addled

red-headed mother everyone
talked about. She was sleeping with
every husband in town, took six men

at once into the Holiday Inn,
waved tornadoes down to ravage
entire suburbs . . . We'd see you

after dinner—after Spaghettios
and Wonder Bread—doing your homework,
grinding it out, your face in shadow.

And what shadows she made through
the rest of the house! Breasts
small or large—we had no comparison—

dipping and rising to the moaning
of the sax, her arms exciting the blue
air. Miles, bashful overachiever,

 straight-A doodler, your owlish gaze
from page 2 fixes me this morning
at the kitchen table. The new

Sonny Rollins, they're calling you.
The Ornette Coleman of the '80s.
Know, as you look into the hazy,

expectant half-drunk faces tonight,
that her every riff and step helped us
discover the tiny dynamos whirring inside

our chests. Know that we loved dying
every night in the flame of her motion.

ON MY 13ᵀᴴ BIRTHDAY MY MOTHER CONVINCES MY FATHER TO SIT DOWN WITH ME AND DISCUSS THE FACTS OF LIFE

Son, he said, in the half shadow
of my bedroom, Bob Cousy
taped to the wall and dribbling toward us,

the early-evening moon smiling
crookedly through the window,
I want to talk with you about

"life," you know—
the birds & bees thing?
You got any questions about that?

Prickles of sweat broke out
above his lip, and he made a steeple
with his stubby fingers. I smoothed

a palm over the hard, raised nubs
of the new Spalding basketball
I'd just unwrapped.

Not really, I said. *Well then*, he added,
Let's go shoot some hoops.

 II.

LAST AT BAT, TEXAS LEAGUE PLAYOFFS, 1961

You hit .219 this year. Congratulations.—my father

The shadows of the light poles
lengthened to meet me at the plate.
All my Rocky Colavito bat and I
had ever wanted was to smack
a Benny Banta fastball and launch
a perfect arc over the left fielder's
astonished head.

All Banta knew was to throw smoke
and mirrors at us, a pack of Camels
and pack of rubbers keeping company
in his back pocket.

I took my closed stance, my knees
castanets: *Strike One.*

I knew Williams's book on hitting
by heart, spent hours studying
the night-shot trajectories in *Life*
of Ewell Blackwell's whiplash curve:
Strike Two.

Banta couldn't have read
The Little Engine That Could
if his curve ball depended on it
(it didn't). He wound up again
like a man with too many arms.

The baseball golf ball aspirin tablet
was past me before I swung
with everything I'd ever learned:
Strike Three.

My father groaned behind the dugout.
Four rows up, the Big League scout
stuck his pencil behind an ear.

I trudged back to the bench,
the Little Engine That Could
Never Get on Track. No one said
a word or sat beside me on that bench
because suddenly my uniform

had turned into a pin-striped suit;
a Windsor knot sprouted a tie
from my throat. My Gil Hodges mitt
fell between my feet
and became a leather briefcase
full of accounts past due, board minutes,
memos from the future.

WHEN I HEARD THE NEWS

Once, driving the small back roads of Kansas
in November, nothing on my mind but the sun
firing through a magnificent spreading oak,
I rounded a curve and a chicken
bloodied my windshield. I couldn't stop it
from happening, the hard, invisible wall
of glass between us. Two feathers
stuck there as I braked, too late.
In the rearview mirror, it struggled
to fluff itself up, then toppled.

I thought to go back. Scoop up
the stopped heart and broken feathers and carry it
to the farmhouse door. But it was only a chicken,
after all, a chicken that had gotten careless
and would have been tied to a clothesline
anyway, to await the swift cleaver.

So I went on down the road in my first car,
1963, sunlight shooting across wheatfields.
When the radio fixed me in that spot forever
with the news from Dallas.

After the Move Back to Wichita

Fall 1964

Phoenix had been hell that summer
and for my father, hell on wheels.
How could he not fail: the new guy
from Kansas making cold calls
in the rusty, shit-green Pioneer Steel
station wagon, AC chugging out
more hot air. The sun was relentless
as the promise he'd made to us:
It's simple, so simple—there's a fortune
to be made out there! And then, day
after day, the blank order pads he'd lug
in from the car. The litany of *nobody*
buying, nobody buying . . .

Back in Wichita, the house we'd left
for a realtor to do his best, my father
knelt over a bucket in the driveway.
He lifted the green hose and watched
water trickle into powdered cement.
He stirred the silicate and aluminate
like a man trying to coax fire from cinders.

When he hobbled toward me,
pulled by the weight of the bucket,
I had already set the last stones
into the knee-high wall outlining
our garden plot. Our Best Boys
would luxuriate, green peppers
fatten in the sun . . .

Dad stretched out on his back
in the center of what we'd built.
He was tired of this, tired now
of everything. He folded his hands
over his chest. He barely breathed.
And I was happy to hear Mother clang

the cowbell for dinner, even though
we'd eat again in silence, the silence
saying that surely the man
who'd brought us this far and back
can find something as simple as a job.

MY SENIOR YEARBOOK PHOTO

First, please excuse
the Goldwater pin. I was
temporarily insane.
The poorly knotted
skinny black tie scissoring
crookedly from my throat?
Dad tied it, so blame him.
But he's not to blame
for the tidal wave
of Brylcreamed hair,
a shiny black tsunami breaking
on the shore of fashion
already out of fashion.
And what to make of this
goofy grin? Who was I
trying to be? Anyone
but myself is the answer.
Someone, perhaps, who could
somehow snuggle between
sultry Cheryl Woodruff
(French Club, 2, 3; After School
Sports 1, 2, 3) and sexy Donna
Wright ("My Three Angels," 3;
Twirler, 1, 2, 3) and make them
smile this way forever.

LEGACY

My father told me he'd show me
something I'd never forget. I was 17.
That's why we were sitting
at the El Pussy Cat,
a Wichita Saturday night.
The air's sweat beaded the glass
lip of my first Black Label.
We were watching Wanda's body
become pure torsion, pure fire.
She rode the smoke-filled air.
She made her tassles snap
like little whips. And a man
who'd been going table to table,
dragging one short foot
behind the other,
tapped the back of my neck
and slid his face close.
His smile was a long blade.
He reached inside a paper bag,
pulled up a handful of glass.
I'll eat this for a dollar
is what he said, as Wanda's
white leather boots strutted
toward me. *I'll crunch it right up*
and swallow for one American dollar.
My father looked hard at me,
an adult in his world now, and nodded.
I slid a bill between the bleeding fingers.

DRIVING LATE TO THE PARTY, 1968

and paying good money
to dodge these turnpike potholes
from Wichita to Lawrence,
a thin drift of fog lifting
around the ten o'clock
whine of the engine,
80 miles an hour,
the last half-inch
of Old Mr. Boston
passing between us
in the confluent haze.
And all these tumbleweeds!
The wind whipping them at us—
pigweed, bugseed,
the stark dry rasp shredding
in the car's wheelwells,
sticking in the Mustang's grille,
one headlight blinded
and still they come,
dozens of wind globes
hurling themselves at us,
the whole prairie coming
undone, scattering
its seed, the turquoise
dashlights flowing
down our cheekbones
as we shoot through
another underpass,
twenty and drunk and itching
just to be there,
blind and ready.

(for G.L. Dold)

BURNOUT

was what the game was called,
the game of catch Dad and I played.
You stand 50 feet away at first

and throw the ball hard as you can
to your partner, your opponent. It's
a dialectic of quick heat. You need

nerves like wrought iron, nimble
reflexes, a well-padded glove.
We had just argued at dinner,

black clouds flexing in the window.
My hair was too long and Dad
demanded to know what was in

the aromatic baggie
he turned up in my glove box.
It was 1969, and he invested

every ounce of righteous energy
he could muster in firing the ball
at me in the backyard. *Tradition*

thunked like a sledgehammer
into my mitt; then *family*,
the American Way. I hurled back

a dorsal-carpel-popping *carpe diem*,
Happy Hour haze, recreational sex.
At 40 feet he wound up like a man

with too many arms, and sent me
reeling on my heels, the ball a spike
in my blistering palm. So I smoked

the next one at his sweaty temple.
Steady job, Dad's return sung out,
the webbing of my Jimmy Piersall

mitt snapping back but holding.
Hedonistic hijinx, I slung back.
Eight-to-five, Albert Camus, credit

rating, Mr. Zig Zag, Windsor knot . . .
With only 30 feet between us, Mother
intervened with two deep blue bowls

of chocolate chip ice cream.
We dropped our steaming gloves
in thick clover. *It's nearly dark*, she said,

someone could get hurt in this game.

FIRST JOB, GRIFF'S BURGER BAR

On the grease-stained tile
    and gray clots of snow
        three men appeared

at closing time. Hoods pulled tight
    around their red faces,
        they looked like monks,

I thought, until the one with fingers
    like raw sausages said
        On the floor. Now.

He held the gun, the fat bullets
    waiting in their round casements.
        I went down

and the manager, Gary, crumpled
    beside the open safe. It was
        New Year's Day, 1965,

and I was scheduled to be off, home
    watching football with my dad,
        Mother in the kitchen

popping popcorn. But I'd filled in
    for Rich, whose wife was due
        any day. Any day now

he'd have a son, someone, it occurred
    to me just then, who could some day
        sidle through a back door

with his buddies and shoot a couple
    of kids brainless enough
        to be working

for a dollar an hour, or shoot them
      for money they didn't have . . .
         I lay face down,

forehead on my forearm and wondered
      how much it would hurt, not
         to be shot but to feel

the butt of the gun indent my skull.
      Eyes closed, I started counting
         the night's take, hoping

it was enough to make them go away.
      When I felt the barrel
         against my neck I thought

to say something to make it disappear,
      and all I could utter, the register
         of my voice climbing

back into childhood, was *Take my wallet,*
      please, sir. An enormous
         silence fell around us.

And when the time clock struck down
      another minute, it was the sound
         of a ball bearing dropped

into a pie pan. I twitched and let loose
      a long stream of air.
         Then my mouth was stopped

with a greasy rag and I was hogtied
      with my own apron string.
         When the police arrived,

our lights blazing long after closing time,
       they put us in a warm car
             and gave us coffee,

and the owner, Mr. Griffith, drove up
       in his bronze Lincoln
             and asked if we were OK,

and hugged us as if we were long-lost
       sons and gave us
             the Christmas bonus

he'd forgotten, twenty dollars.
       His wife, Tracy, kissed me
             on the forehead and stroked

my cheek, and Gary, who'd never uttered
       a kind word to me, said we'd go
             for a beer after work next Friday,

that he'd buy the first round.
       I drove home knowing
             I'd just had the best day of my life.

OUT WITH THE BOYS, WICHITA, 1969

I don't think there were three words in my head yet.
--C.K. Williams, "The Gas Station"

My buddies and I were out after
second shift and a night of drinking.
We were utterly thoughtproof,
stupid with girls, stupid with the bodies
we were trying to grow into.
Blaring the Stones, a percussion
of empty Black Labels under the seat,
I rattled up to crumbling Riverside Zoo.
Derek, already in the duck cage,
had chased down a clipped mallard
and held it aloft like a trophy.
It was blue-black, iridescent.
He cocked it by his right ear,
smoothed the animal into a football.
Jerry, who would be fired from
the print shop six weeks later, ran
out for the pass, which sailed into
the purple night. The bird half-wobbled,
half-flew beyond Jerry's stretch,
over and into the alligator pen.
The duck made the smallest splash
I'd ever heard. It bobbed like a cork
on the water, thinking—however ducks
might think of anything—that this had
turned out all right, its feathers
settling back along its haunches
in smooth moonlight. But then the water
opened wide; the definitive lid of darkness
slammed down.
          Our hands heavy as plumb bobs,
we stood around the cage, reckoning
some depth none of us could fathom.

BOEING PRINT SHOP

I ran a Multilith, 20-year-old ink-
slinging monster that liked to suck
the thin Itek plate into the rollers
and set it flapping like
a storm-blown window shade.

I was making three sixty-five an hour
after a boost from Mr. Masters,
who liked me because I helped his son,
on company time, write book reports.

My first summer there, '68,
the AC out, hundreds of flies invaded
the shop through propped-open windows.
Bored, we'd blast them with rubber bands
and tally the daily body count.

Richard killed 34 during one slow shift
in July. Jerry Calvert took the record
for distance, smashing one from 25 ½ feet,
and Terry won Most Memorable Kill,
nailing a couple mating nine feet up.

Most amazing to me, Mr. Masters
didn't seem to notice an entire wall
of his shop turning into a pointillist painting,
or the body parts lining the baseboard—
vellum wings, legs, a scramble of antennae . . .

Five gooks at one o'clock, Emmett would say
from the Itek machine, and we'd idle our presses
long enough to surprise the squadron of flies.

It got us through the night, I guess,
through those long shifts before Emmett
was drafted and passed the piss test
in Kansas City and found himself
in boot camp "too exhausted to be terrified."
He wrote one short note, then nobody heard.

So I upped my eight hours a semester to 12.
I locked myself in a bathroom stall
and spent company time reading
the tissue-paper pages of the *Norton Anthology*:
I will show you fear in a handful of dust.

When news came that Emmett had been killed
his second day in country on something called
the Sihonouk Trail, Mr. Masters gathered us
for a moment of silence. Ethel cried at her press.
Richard checked a tear beside me. And Jerry and I,
the next Saturday, came in on our own time

with brushes and buckets and sponges. We scraped
the wall top to bottom until no trace remained
of our carnage, swept the bodies and parts of bodies
into a dustpan . . .

We showed the guard our badges, and stepped
into the parking lot. The lights snapped on, nodding
on their long spindles, and fixed us there.

HOW TO BECOME A PROFESSIONAL FOLK SINGER

at the newly opened Ambush Club, Wichita, 1971

There I was: lemon-tinted Lennon glasses,
paisley shirt like ironed vomit, corroded
toenails dangling from K-Mart sandals . . .

And when Otis Redding was cut off mid-chorus
from the juke, the three dozen dressed-to-the-max
black couples gazed up at me, each mouth a rictus,

as I tuned my Yamaha in the circle of light.
Close enough for folk music, I declared
and began to strum my three-chord version

of Dock of the Bay, a clever segue and nod to Otis,
I thought. My fingers meated through the song.
I sat on that dock watching the waves come and go

through three choruses, then plunked a final major C
with all the majesty of a hammered thumbnail.
And I saw I had stunned the crowd to silence.

Did these fine people think I was a novelty act?
If I'd expected applause, I got a voice in the back saying,
Whoa, Momma—turn on the fire hose.

And poor Dennis, the new owner and dead-ringer
Ozzie Nelson who'd heard me strum "Stewball"
and "Puff" at the Riverside Park Folk Jamboree,

who thought I was good and knew he needed music,
was frozen behind the bar, lava lamps auguring his future:
purple bubbles rising and breaking apart

like the opening-night crowd. The juke erupted
with Otis, back on his dock. The stage lights dimmed.
Drinks on the house! I heard a voice say, Dennis' voice,

and he pressed a twenty into my right palm. *Just go,*
he said. *OK?* I slung the guitar over my shoulder.
He opened the back door to the parking lot,

and I took my rightful place among the stars.

 III.

EUROPE ON $5 A DAY

Then there was the time
      my good friend Lynn Dold and I were hitching
through Europe, '69, summer of the moon landing.
      We'd been standing two kilometers north of Florence
for three and a half hours, sunning our thumbs,
      Frommer's *Europe on $5 a Day*
tucked under my arm like a talisman.

Not one Alfa or lorrie seemed to notice
      the plastic American flag I'd stuck in the top
of my straw hat, when a gray Renault
      pulls over and the doors fly open
and it's *Ili! You're Americans! We're Arnie and Anise
      from Buffalo, New York, and we just landed
yesterday and –hey—hop in!*

Arnie told us he was a dentist (*But you've got nothing
      to fear from me*) and Anise looked like a prize
Pekinese, right down to the pink bow cocked
      over her left ear, turning to say
Hey! We brought Pringles! And cornflakes!
      So there we were heading north to Bologna and on
to Milan, stuffing ourselves with Pringles and corn flakes

and washing it all down with warm cokes which,
      believe me, was fine, was more than fine
after the Italian sun had spent all afternoon
      etching itself into our pink foreheads.
We'd eaten nothing that day but black exhaust
      from potato trucks, one driver pumping us
the good old American finger as he passed, and we must have

dozed in the backseat, slept like Arnie and Anise's
      junk-food-happy teenage kids, because suddenly
there we were at the Swiss border! And for the next 40 miles

it was Arnie and Anise sparring and seeing how much
venom could be pumped into the language: *You changed way too
     many dollars back there, Arnie honey. Well, darling, you
may not have noticed, but we're in a whole other* country *now,*

we might just need *Swiss money here. What am I supposed to do
     with 800,000 frickin lira, Mr. Finance Whiz?
Do you imagine no one in Switzerland is capable of changing
     money from the country right next door, honey?
Just put a cork in the bung hole, Arnie darling.*
And we realized we'd been taken prisoner,
unwitting witnesses to a marriage falling away

like the red-striped mileposts. They bickered all the way
     to the Matterhorn, and as Arnie torqued up
the mountain on the thin two-lane, Anise's mother—*poof!*—
     was sitting on my lap, her scowl and bad breath,
her constant nagging making Arnie want to *part her hair
     with an ax* and there was Arnie's 300-pound dad
joining us in the back, too, eating a popcorn ball:

*Oh, I'll talk about your dear old dad all I like, Arnie.
     Just like you, he's got the personality of a mush melon . . ..*
And as we rounded a tight curve at 73 km an hour,
     she slapped him—slapped our driver!—and all of us
in the back seat cowered and covered our heads and knew
     we were going over and down 6,880 feet,
especially after Arnie freed his hands of the wheel and slapped

a string of blood from Anise's nose. Then, looking over his
     shoulder at me from the front seat, black-hooded
and grinning, was *Death,* extending a bony hand my way
     as in the oncoming lane a tour bus—thank god
a tour bus—was bearing down and righted Arnie for the moment.
     His foot lifted from the pedal and moved

to the brake, and we were so goddamned happy

to get out on the flower-laden side of that mountain, and leave
        Arnie and Anise and their in-laws to squabble it out
that we nearly floated two miles uphill to the nearest pizzeria
        and promptly drank down six dark beers.
We were a short train ride from Geneva, where we'd buddy up
        with three Canadians and sneak into the Hotel Du Rhone
and get arrested the next morning for art theft.

        But that's another story.

SOFT LANDINGS
for SP

We lay naked on the pliant roof of your VW van,
imagining, beyond the cottonwoods,
the moon landing.

Apollo was snug in the Sea of Tranquility.
Armstrong and Buzz and the boys,
feeling impossibly lucky,

lowered the lunar ladder and broke the surface.
Which is when you began humming
the theme from "Mission Impossible"

and climbed onto me, lucky me, mosquitoes revving
their little motors around us,
looking for a world to touch down on.

A cloud passed over the moon at the first kiss
 of space boots on astral soil.
 My fingertips traced the constellation

of freckles on your shoulder. The radio crackled
touchdown as, through whoops and applause,
I bent up to lick an eyelid open.

We would want our eyes open for this,
the roof of the world off at last.

DURING A ZEN READING
MY LIBIDO ACTS UP AGAIN

after Lucien Stryk

In the crowded room
you spoke slowly, calmly,
of the Zen Master

who sat silent for days
staring at bamboo
until finally he felt

he became bamboo
and bamboo
became himself.

I tried to concentrate
but sitting in front
of me, dazed,

was a girl whose hair
was the color of wheat:
it hung down

the back of her chair
running in and out
of itself

and in again,
braided tight and thick
and balancing on my

hospitable knees. Then,
like a young mare waking
from a doze of sunlight,

she shook her head.
A single strand
floated up,

curled through the bamboo-
scented air, and landed
like an invitation

in my open palm.

(Wichita State, 1974)

LOADED

for Janice B

We'd just had lackluster sex
in her father's bedroom
and were talking about the war
our fathers fought,
gin slurring to *gun* at 2 a.m.
Her dad had stripped a Nazi
of his Luger (*or so he claims,* Janice
said). The stainless steel lock
on the ancient attic trunk
fell away and Janice dredged the dark
prize up to the light. The one thing
in the world she knew for sure
just then was that the gun wasn't loaded.
She sighted down the long black barrel
and found my forehead. Did I mention
bad sex? She laughed and went *pooosh!--*
squeezing off an imaginary round, then
set the Luger down. When the gun went off
we jumped. Three long seconds hung
heavy as lead between us. And my left big toe
was smoking! We looked down—
my toe was on fire!
            No: the smoke, we saw then,
was merely dust the bullet had prized up
from the floorboards. What could we do
but laugh? Janice slipped the Luger back
in its holster and shut the trunk.
We were done with war stories.
Her father wouldn't be home for hours.

SLEEPING WITH TWO WOMEN

As I remember it, we emptied
three bottles of Mateus
and wedged ourselves

onto their third-story windowsill.
We watched the snow pile up
around us, one fat rectangular flake

after another shuffling down
to erase every step we'd taken,
my '59 Chevy disappearing

under a helmet of snow.
We had time for such deliberate
watching then, Wichita, 1968.

And I remember us laughing
about Sharon's ex—a guy
who kept tires in their bedroom—

and Barbara's story of the time
she slept with her brother
on a family vacation in Minnesota:

Here, feel this, he said, Barbara
screaming at her first encounter
with a boner, but laughing now.

The snow kept tumbling down,
and I don't know who suggested it,
but I remember the slow undressing

as if we were figures being carved
in ivory. The candle in the bedroom
strobed light onto the lip of the bottle

I was holding like a trophy. And when
Barbara's panties finally fell away
like a white petal, we all piled into bed

laughing at our nakedness—
no rippling muscles, not a sculpted
buttock among us. I nudged in

between them, and what happened
in that bed, under the Niagara of snow,
candlelight drawing hieroglyphs

on the walls, was simply that they inched
toward me, close enough so that
we were touching but not touching.

Perhaps passion flared up in some other
candlelit room that night. Here,
I reached out my hands and felt them

settle, lightly (forty heartbeats or so
away from sleep), on those warm separate
continents. Perfectly at home, perfectly lost.

CHERYL LEIGH, I THINK
HER NAME WAS

Wichita, 1968

I went to bed once with a woman
I didn't love, didn't even like, because
she could name every Brooklyn Dodger

on the '55 team. I overlooked the Nixon
button that clasped her cleavage,
and the fact that she drank Black Label,

in cans. In her bedroom, our clothes floated off
like ghosts in dim lamplight. She chanted *Reese,
Robinson, Snider*; I tossed back *Campanella,*

Hodges, Furillo. Newcombe, Erskine, she breathed
into my ear, *Podres, Loes,* I breathed back. Then
we went into the bull pen for *Spooner, Labine*

and *Roebuck.* But by the time we got to the end
of the dugout bench (Bob Borkowski slumped
hopelessly in the shadows), she realized

she couldn't do it after all, not with somebody
whose car sported a Humphrey sticker,
somebody who'd opened the barroom window

and poured her Black Label into the weeds . . .
So I didn't slide home safely (cf., Robinson, game 1,
8th inning, World Series); instead, I found myself out

in her driveway, finished for the night
with the national pastime. And drove home
with the boys of summer in the dawn's early light.

JOY

Maybe it's always mixed,
like with Sally in '74,

who touched me more tenderly
and convincingly

than any woman had, then spent
half an hour of pillow talk

on the Etruscans,
the Tarquin kings' iron-hand rule

in the latter half
of the 6th century.

The half pound of licorice whips
(I was 7) pulled up two teeth

the same afternoon I jerked
a snapping turtle from the canal

on a cane pole, thrilled until
I looked down to see a leech,

like a blob of cold liver,
sucking my ankle red.

Unadulterated joy? My friend
Lynn and I win the Kansas

Juniors Bowling Tournament in '65
and are handed trophies—

I'm not exaggerating—the size
of salt and pepper shakers.

He glued his plastic bowler next to
his steering wheel, a dashboard

Jesus of Bowling,
until a banana-yellow Corvette

slammed into his Mustang
and broke his trophy in two.

Bad luck? Well, joy can walk
the other side of the street, too:

The Vette belonged to
one Annette Winthrop Vickers,

who took my friend home
and asked his forgiveness

for two months. The Germans
have a word, *Schadenfreude*,

for another kind of joy:
the evangelist caught

with his pants down in the choir loft,
or the child molester trapped

in the burning Tunnel of Love . . .
To look and have one more look,

Lot's wife notwithstanding,
is also a kind of joy, the slugger

whizzing one an inch the wrong side
of the foul pole, then settling

in the box again. The next pitch
is a lollypop in his sweet zone;

he tenses his biceps, undercuts
the fat curve and like Isabella

waving Chris Columbus
over the horizon watches it

sail out of sight . . .
It plops into the glove of

Candi McFarland, celebrating
her 10th birthday. She can't

believe it; she can't believe it!
She had her eyes closed! Joy,

a small hard sphere, turns
now in her hand, a new world

she holds up for everyone to see,
her glove hand, for weeks,

stinging gloriously.

MR. PEANUT

An undergrad down on my luck, dead broke, I suited up in a back
room of Wichita's new mall. The promise of twenty dollars put
me in a gold-brown Latex suit with little raised bumps suggesting,
I imagined, the nubs on the shell. Black pointy shoes with white
spats, black wooden cane and top hat, bright white Mickey Mouse
gloves . . . I was just tying on my cardboard peanut mask when
a girl rushed into the room and took off her sombrero, her hair
a dark velvet waterfall, and began changing out of her Mexican
food outfit. But before she could wiggle out of her huipil, she
screamed, because a human peanut was lurching toward her,
replete with white plastic monocle covering one eye. I was half
blind so had to ask her to please please hand me my peanut-shaped
basket full of giveaway bags, which she did pronto since, clearly,
she wanted me as far away as I could take my stupid peanut self
. . . I managed to find the snack section and began doing a little
impromptu peanut dance. I hummed something (I think it was
"These Boots Are Made for Walking"). An avuncular legume, I
tipped my hat to the ladies; I handed out free stuff to the kids
and their moms, who smiled at me. And I have to say I was
kind of getting into it, the congenial peanut full of freebies and
good wishes, kids now flocking around me like I was Jesus curing
walk-in lepers, dispensing peanuts like the pope proffering wafers,
which is exactly when my mask popped loose and toppled into a
woman's cart . . . So Mr. Peanut was, after all, just some kid with a
scruffy black beard, a little drunk, perhaps, some ridiculous hybrid
whose white gloves and white spats, under the intense neon, now
seemed somehow perverse. Moms shooed away their kids, and of
course at that exact moment the girl who'd just broken up with
me, one Darlene Diehl by name, rounded the corner into Snacks.
She fixed me with a look that told the whole store, the whole

world, *Christ, I sure made the right call this time*, and I just stood there, a human malaprop, a scarecrow stuck into Antarctic ice, as the Napoleonic assistant manager strode down the aisle. *What the hey, new boy?* he said. Then he was pointing to the dressing room. I knew there would be no twenty dollars. And as I trudged home through the slush-pocked snow, coat pockets bulging with the packets, it occurred to me that I was a man who would probably, forever and always, work for peanuts.

SO YOU WANT TO BE A TEACHING ASSISTANT IN ENGLISH

Rent a tiny room half a mile from campus.
It will be winter, and all winter long
your radiator will be a cold slab of ribs.
Worse, it's Wichita, or somewhere
not much better, and you were dealt
a 7 a.m. class.
                    On the sidewalk you move
in your monstrous coat like a moonwalker.
You follow the bouncing full moon
of your flashlight, like the dim beam
on a miner's helmet, leading you
to English 101, Fiske Hall. Shivering
in their coats, the 28 students hate you
because it's your fault the afternoon classes
were full. They hate you because it's Wichita
and their hair is frozen to their heads.
And they really hate this first assignment—
Write about your most intense personal experience—
because their most intense personal experiences
were lips-stuck-to-frozen-lampposts
kinds of things, or, worse, they're still waiting
for an intense moment to occur to them,
some razory lightning bolt of experience
to rearrange their bland circuitry.
                    And you—you're only a few years older
than them anyway and still don't understand
the difference between a restrictive
and nonrestrictive clause so who are you—
unzippering your briefcase like their father
home from work—to dispense these nuggets
of wisdom you've pirated from Strunk and White . . .
                    You return
double-spaced confessions to Kathys
and Karens and Jims who are simply
hoping to have something come back

without much blood spilled on it,
something that maybe you've even pronounced
Good! or *Shows some potential.*
                    But now you see Julie
in the corner staring at the circled D+, her rambling
rendition of the unhappy tryst between her dachshund
and a Mack truck, and she begins to cry, audibly,
because she'd poured her heart out and—OK—
there were fragments and run-ons and she just can't get
the difference between there and their and they're,
but her dog Fritz was, after all, an A+ kind of dog,
which should count for something, right? *Why,* her tears
seem to be asking, *did I have to get a teacher who hates dogs
so much?* And she leaves the classroom, shutting the door
gently, before you can think what to do. Perhaps
she'll go hang herself or, worse, report you,
and you know you've got nothing the next hour
but a drill on dangling modifiers and ice
is etching little flowers on the windows
and now you've got to pee, and when it gets dead
quiet in the room and you're standing there
with your tongue puddling in your mouth,
and half the students are eyeing the door Julie
escaped through, you realize, finally,
what it's like to be in charge.

IV.

SKUNK

Evening drifts in with a wave
        of skunk, then mimosa,
then—unmistakable now—

skunk. I hear something
        gutteral next door—
all the hard dog consonants

grinding the air. The sun
        is almost down. Birds
stop bickering in the trees.

And now I see the skunk, sticking
        its blunt snout
out of the bank of coreopsis

along our fence and sniffing
        the air. I've
never seen a skunk in the city,

though I've driven its stink
        for miles
along maize and wheatfields,

not knowing whether to roll
        the windows up or down.
I'm close enough now to hit it

with this empty beer bottle,
        the fat skunk body
having emerged from the flowers,

its glossy back iridescent
        in the late pink
slant of sun. And I think

of my father's breath
        the one time
I saw him drunk, years before

shrapnel began to cut its way
        out of his legs,
before vertigo leveled him

to a recliner and daily Cubs' game.
        It was summer.
He slammed the back screen

and rushed inside. His breath
        was a fusillade of whisky,
his eyes monstrous lakes a boy

could drown in. He lifted me up
        before I could run
and took me outside, the night

thick with fireflies. We sat
        in silence. The pulse
of the wind beat in my ear.

I didn't know what was wrong
        but understood
he needed this silence

to be enormous, a storehouse
        for something gnawing
and growing inside him . . .

The skunk, meanwhile, has spotted me
        in the lawn chair.
He might think, *This is something*

large that can hurt, it doesn't
           want me here.
The bottle misses him, his tail

a ragged plume of smoke
           rounding the corner.
He was right, and is already

someplace else, wrapping
           the darkness around him,
settling into what is irrevocably his.

HERE IS MY FATHER

at 25, in his sergeant's stripes, smiling at the camera with my mother.
They're back from their honeymoon in Colorado Springs.
Cottonwood fuzz swirls around them like confetti.

at 40, at his punch press in the garage. I'm handing him a brown
envelope from Washington containing Dad's patent for
the "Worley Collapsible Redwood Tomato Stake."

at 7, wearing knickers, his ears propping up a tam-o'-shanter.
Snowball, a white blur, sits on his lap. Eight years later
he will back over her in the gravel driveway.

at 50, back in the kitchen after excusing himself from his birthday
party. He's wearing full Indian headdress; he's painted his
face red. He stands in silence and won't explain.

at 35, coming through the front door with a stack of order forms
from his western Kansas circuit. He's just sold $3,000 worth
of steel in one week. We all dine out at McDonald's.

at 65, Las Vegas, behind a small pyramid of blue and red chips at
the Golden Nugget. He slowly turns over the fourth 9 to beat
some loud Oklahoman's full boat. I am so happy, I whoop.

at 23, lying in the pink snow. A blond SS soldier points a rifle
at his head as blood seeps from Dad's knee and ankle.
The moon, bone white, drifts through black branches.

at 76, in the Tucson Care Facility. The night nurse finds him, naked
and trembling, standing by the bedside of a Mrs Wolcott.
He thinks she is his mother.

at 33, in the Wesley Hospital elevator, his face backlit with joy. He
tells me I have another baby brother, named Steven.
I follow his limp to the Maternity Ward.

at 71, guiding his '59 Cadillac onto a ramp marked DO NOT ENTER.
Pull over, I say. *Now. OK*, he says—
You drive the rest of the way.

LETTER I NEVER SENT MY FATHER

First, I want to say that most of the advice you gave me
was useful as a pocket watch dipped into molasses.
About girls: *Never kiss them before they're ready.*
And later that same night sweet Darlene held out

her hand to me: *Blotter acid,* she said, *I've already
taken mine.* But I loved, when you came home from work,
the anachronistic way you'd shoot hoops in your coat and tie,
bucket-style, scooping the ball into the redolent autumn air,
the leather spinning—improbably—through the net.

My first night drunk, on my knees in the damp basement,
tomato beer and Mogen David rollicking in my guts,
you watched from the top step as I shot prodigious volleys
of what must have looked to you like blood
before you spotted the empty Mad Dog bottle.

Think you'll live? you shouted down, and let me continue
meting out my own punishment while you made us coffee.
I loved it when you'd take me along on your calls—

to Fergusen Tool and Die in Ulysses, Tumbleweed Steel
in Great Bend, Western Kansas flat as the one draft
you'd buy me later, Black Label, Schlitz . . .

And then we'd go to the Elk's or VFW in whatever town,
where you'd sit with strangers and toss dollar bills and fives
onto green felt. In Syracuse one night you hit a boat

on the last card, and let me peek at that sweet king of hearts.
I hushed back in the shadows. A man nearly twice your size
stood, and flopped five diamonds. When your trip kings

and sixes exploded up at him like an aurora borealis,
he reached across the table and grabbed your collar.
Bucko, you said, *you don't know what kind of hardware*

*I'm holding down here in my coat pocket. Goddamn lucky
bastard!* the man yelled, slamming the door behind him. You
blew out a puff of air, stood, and turned your coat pockets

inside out. Then you let me rake the pot.

MY MOTHER'S 85ᵀᴴ BIRTHDAY

From her early instruction
I know the knife and spoon
go on the right, fork on the left.
The covered wagon riding the center
of each plate should be right-side up,
of course, the full, bone-white moon
in its rightful corner.

Instead of grace, I sing Happy Birthday,
Mother tapping out the trochaic
with her spoon here in assisted living
where women come and go to help
ensure her small comforts. And I recall
this day exactly 50 years ago: all morning

I sat at our mahogany dining room table,
polishing my mother's commemorative spoons.
It was my job to make them shine.
I set them on the Sunday funnies side
by side, squirted a clean cloth with Wright's,
and began.

I burnished the scowling face of Sitting Bull,
felt the weight of the West settle into my palm,
Bill Cody bagging the last buffalo.
I rubbed the Kansas City stockyards clean,

waxed Ike's bald head, buffed thick stalks
of wheat on the decorative handle
of The Reaper, walking toward sunset
with his wife and his sickle.

I scoured the luxuriant tarnished beard
of Whitman, scrubbed in the cradle
of the spoon my own too-serious face.

I smoothed the rag across letters that rose
from the bowl of the spoon to build
Bridgeport, CONN, curlicues rising
and falling like thin whips up the shaft
to the chiseled face of P.T. Barnum.

I set each in its niche in the long
wooden rack. Then the relatives,
like a circus troupe, arrived—

From the street the slamming
of car doors—*Goddamn Democrats,*
Goddamn Democrats, Dean's Sunday
litany rolling toward us like a runaway boulder,

Uncle Jack with the gin rickey jitters,
Aunt Wilda, perfume a mix
of honeysuckle and turpentine.
Violet with the wild blue hair, and
Aunt Kay, pulling Uncle Matt behind her
like a wagonload of dread.
Phil and Kent and P.K., the skinny
crewcut cousins, tried to become invisible,
slinking into the rec room shadows,
the whole Worley genepool swirling
through our house like a chaotic microcosmos.

Then everyone filed by Peg's spoons,
admiring the two new ones,
each face in each tiny concavity
a dark inverted moon. We sat.
Uncle Paul offered a prayer,
a brief respite of silence

before Dean described, in detail,
his recent appendectomy,
Paul countered with his ongoing battle
against "explosive bowel syndrome,"
Violet stood to show off
the scar traversing her right thigh
after the "hedge clipper incident," and
Wilda did a paradiddle on her empty wine glass
for attention before clicking out
a whole row of teeth—the family history
of misery accompanied for nearly two hours
by the clatter of silverware, the tinkle
of crystal as wine bottles made their rounds,
Matt finally deciding to hold up his end
of the conversation by blowing a gaseous
cloud over all of us from a freshly lit cigar . . .

Now, at her small kitchen table, Mother
and I share this memory. She lifts
her yearly glass of red wine, and we drink
a toast to the simple, miraculous fact of still
being here. Along the long wall above us
her spoons, in their proper places, shining.

I would like to thank The Kentucky Arts Council for two Al Smith Fellowships that supported the writing of many of these poems, and the Lexington-Frankfort poetry group—Richard Taylor, Marcia Hurlow, Leatha Kendrick, Tom Webster, Mike Moran, Dave Cazden, and Susan Cobin—for their invaluable attention to early drafts of many of these poems. And to my good poet-folksinger friend Mike Schneider for his astute readings and helpful suggestions. And to first-rate novelist Gaylord Lynn Dold, who was there at the inception of this book and helped convince me to try to move it on down the road. And Izzy Wasserstein at Woodley Press for the sharp editorial suggestions.

And a special loving thanks to Linda for her smart reading of early drafts and her continuous and sustaining support.

— *Jeff Worley*

About the Author

Born and raised in Wichita, Kansas, Jeff Worley was the second graduate of the Wichita State University MFA program in 1975. He won the Mid-List Press First-Book Poetry Prize for *The Only Time There Is*, and his second book from Mid-List, *Happy Hour at the Two Keys Tavern*, was awarded the 2006 Kentucky Book of the Year Prize in Poetry and named co-winner in the 2007 Society of Midland Authors Literary Competition. He has also published two books of poems from Larkspur Press in Monterey, Kentucky: *Best to Keep Moving* and *A Simple Human Motion*. Worley also served as editor of the anthology *What Comes Down to Us: 25 Contemporary Kentucky Poets*, which was published by the University Press of Kentucky in 2009.

His poems have appeared in many literary magazines and journals over the years, including *College English*, *The Threepenny Review*, *Poetry Northwest*, *Chicago Review*, *The Georgia Review*, *Boulevard*, *New England Review*, *Shenandoah*, *The Southern Review*, *The Missouri Review*, and *New Letters*.

Now retired from the University of Kentucky, he lives in Lexington with his wife, Linda, and their two cats.